NORTH AMERICAN ANIMALS

Common Snapping Turtles

by Rebecca Sabelko

BELLWETHER MEDIA • MINNEAPOLIS, MN

Note to Librarians, Teachers, and Parents:

Blastoff! Readers are carefully developed by literacy experts and combine standards-based content with developmentally appropriate text.

Level 1 provides the most support through repetition of high-frequency words, light text, predictable sentence patterns, and strong visual support.

Level 2 offers early readers a bit more challenge through varied simple sentences, increased text load, and less repetition of high-frequency words.

Level 3 advances early-fluent readers toward fluency through increased text and concept load, less reliance on visuals, longer sentences, and more literary language.

Level 4 builds reading stamina by providing more text per page, increased use of punctuation, greater variation in sentence patterns, and increasingly challenging vocabulary.

Level 5 encourages children to move from "learning to read" to "reading to learn" by providing even more text, varied writing styles, and less familiar topics.

Whichever book is right for your reader, Blastoff! Readers are the perfect books to build confidence and encourage a love of reading that will last a lifetime!

This edition first published in 2019 by Bellwether Media, Inc.

No part of this publication may be reproduced in whole or in part without written permission of the publisher. For information regarding permission, write to Bellwether Media, Inc., Attention: Permissions Department, 6012 Blue Circle Drive, Minnetonka, MN 55343.

Library of Congress Cataloging-in-Publication Data

Names: Sabelko, Rebecca, author.
Title: Common Snapping Turtles / by Rebecca Sabelko.
Description: Minneapolis, MN : Bellwether Media, Inc., 2019. | Series:
   Blastoff! Readers. North American Animals | Audience: Age 5-8. | Audience:
   K to Grade 3. | Includes bibliographical references and index.
Identifiers: LCCN 2018030419 (print) | LCCN 2018032389 (ebook) | ISBN
   9781681036427 (ebook) | ISBN 9781626179110 (hardcover : alk. paper)
Subjects: LCSH: Chelydra serpentina–Juvenile literature. | Snapping turtles–Juvenile literature.
Classification: LCC QL666.C539 (ebook) | LCC QL666.C539 S23 2019 (print) |
   DDC 597.92/2–dc23
LC record available at https://lccn.loc.gov/2018030419

Editor: Kate Moening   Designer: Josh Brink

Printed in the United States of America, North Mankato, MN.

Table of
Contents

Common snapping turtles are **reptiles** with strong, snapping **jaws**. They spend most of their time in rivers, lakes, and ponds.

4

In the Wild

N
W E
S

Extinct

Extinct in the Wild

Critically Endangered

Endangered

Vulnerable

Near Threatened

Least Concern

common snapping turtle range = ☐
conservation status: least concern

These **solitary** turtles are found throughout the eastern and central United States. They live in southeastern Canada, too.

Common snapping turtles spend summers looking for food in muddy, plant-filled water.

They **hibernate** from late fall to spring. They rest in mud, under logs, or in the homes of other animals.

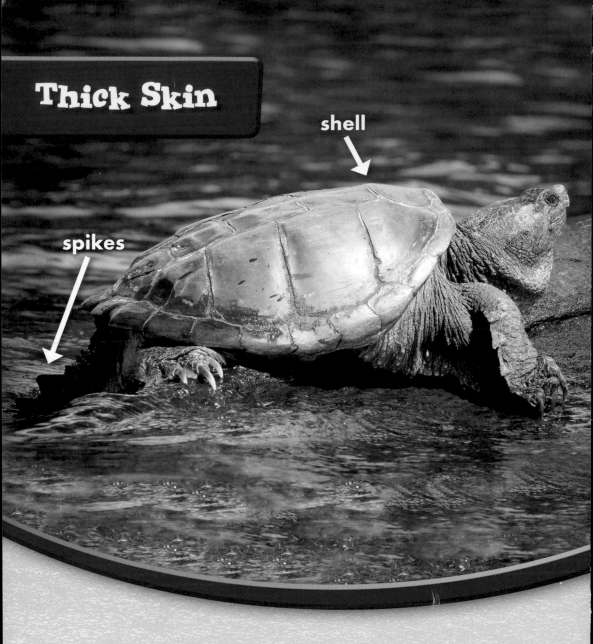

Thick Skin

shell

spikes

Common snapping turtles have hard shells. These are around 8 to 12 inches (20 to 30 centimeters) long.

Size of a Common Snapping Turtle

average human

common snapping turtle

6
5
4
3
2
1
(feet)

Their tails are as long as their shells. Tails are covered in sharp **spikes**.

Common snapping turtles' lower shells make a cross shape. The turtles cannot hide their heads and legs!

lower shell

tubercles

Identify a Common Snapping Turtle

long spiked tail

rough upper shell

hooked jaw

Their legs and necks are covered in rough **tubercles**. These help the turtles feel what is around them.

Common snapping turtles
swim slowly to find food.
They use their senses of
smell, sight, and touch.

They also wait for **prey** to come to them. Their strong, beak-like jaws snap at animals passing by.

On the Menu

green algae

mink frogs

eastern newts

muckets

These **omnivores** like to eat
meat more than plants.
But they will eat whatever
they can fit into their jaws!

Common snapping turtles often swallow food whole. They use their front claws to break large prey into smaller bites.

Animals to Avoid

American alligators

great blue herons

striped skunks

northern water snakes

Common snapping turtles are often **aggressive** when they are not in water. This keeps **predators** away.

When in water, these turtles hide in mud. Only their noses and eyes stay uncovered.

Hatchlings on the Loose

nest

Female common snapping turtles leave the water to lay eggs. They dig a nest in a sunny spot using their back legs. Then, they lay around 40 eggs and bury them in the nest.

Baby Facts

Name for babies:	hatchlings
Number of eggs laid:	up to 40
Time spent inside egg:	75 to 95 days
Time spent with mom:	1 day

Soon, **hatchlings** use **egg teeth** and claws to break out of their eggs!

The hatchlings make their way
to the closest body of water.
They have found a new home!

Glossary

aggressive—showing a readiness to fight

egg teeth—special teeth baby common snapping turtles use to break out of an egg; an egg tooth is on the outside of the jaw.

hatchlings—baby common snapping turtles

hibernate—to spend the winter sleeping or resting

jaws—the two bones of the face that open and close for holding or crushing something

omnivores—animals that eat both plants and animals

predators—animals that hunt other animals for food

prey—animals that are hunted by other animals for food

reptiles—cold-blooded animals that have backbones and lay eggs

solitary—living alone

spikes—parts that are very pointed

tubercles—small bumps on plants or animals

To Learn More

AT THE LIBRARY
Baxter, Bethany. *Snapping Turtles*. New York, N.Y.: PowerKids Press, 2014.

Freeman, Debby. *Turtle*. New York, N.Y.: Bearport Publishing, 2017.

Jacobson, Bray. *Reptile Life Cycles*. New York, N.Y.: Gareth Stevens Publishing, 2018.

ON THE WEB

FACTSURFER

Factsurfer.com gives you a safe, fun way to find more information.

1. Go to www.factsurfer.com.

2. Enter "common snapping turtles" into the search box.

3. Click the "Surf" button and select your book cover to see a list of related web sites.

Index

The images in this book are reproduced through the courtesy of: looderoo, front cover (turtle); Karol Kozlowski, front cover (log); Ray Hennessy, pp. 4-5; Ethan Daniels/ WaterFrame/ agefotostock, p. 6; Ethan Daniels, p. 7; purejoyimagery, pp. 8-9; George Gral/ Getty Images, pp. 10-11; Arvind Balaraman, pp. 11 (top left, top right, middle); JG Photo, p. 11 (top middle); KIKE CALVO/ Alamy, pp. 12, 16-17; Zigmund Leszczynski/ agefotostock, p. 13 (turtle); Kinagra, p. 13 (murky water) Chad Zuber, p. 14 (top left); Michiel de Wit, pp. 14 (top right), 16 (bottom right); Jason Patrick Ross, p. 14 (bottom left); zcw, p. 14 (bottom right); Ryan M. Bolton/ Alamy, p. 15; reptiles4all, p. 16 (top left); Tathoms, p. 16 (top right); Eric Isselee, p. 16 (bottom left); Scott Leslie/ Biosphoto, pp. 18-19; Tammy Wolfe/ Alamy, p. 19 (turtle); nasidastudio, p. 19 (rock); Don Johnston/ Getty Images, p. 20; Chris Hill, p. 21.